Argentine Spanish on the Go

An Introduction for Beginners and Novices

by

David S. Luton

Table of Contents

4

Pronunciación

In Spanish, each vowel has only one sound:

a – as in *father*
e – as in *they*
i – as in *police*
o – as in *go*
u – as in *rude*

Consonants

The following consonants in Argentine Spanish are pronounced the same (more or less) as in English: b, d, f, k, l, m, n, p, t

Here are some notable differences:

c – like and *s* if followed by and *e* or *i (cebolla, gracias)*,
otherwise like a *k*, (acción, va*c*a, lo*c*o, *c*ulebra)
ch – like the *ch* of *church*, **never** as in *ache* (*ch*ino, gazpa*ch*o)
cua – like *quah* (*cuá*ndo, *cuá*l)
cue – like *quay* (*cue*llo)
cui - like *quee* (*cui*dado)
cuo – come *quo* (*cuo*ta)
g – like an *h* when followed by an *e* or *i* (*g*eneral, *g*inebra), otherwise like *g* as in *go* (*g*ol)
gue – like *gay* or like *ge* as in *get* (*gue*to)
gui – like *ghee* (*gui*tarra)
güe – like *gway* (bilin*güe*)
h – always silent (*h*ola)
j – always like an English *h* (*J*uan)

5

ll – like the *s* in the word *measure*

ñ – like *ny* in the word *canyon* (*lasaña*)

que – like *kay* (*qué, porque*)

qui – like *key* (*quién, quitar*)

r – not at all like an American *r*, perhaps like the r of the word *very* when pronounced by someone from England

rr – A double *r* (or a single *r* as the first letter of a word or name) will always be trilled or rolled, the same as in Italian. (*arroz, rico, Roberto*)

s – always *ss* sound as in the word *class*, **never** a *z* sound as in the word *nose*

v – In proper Spanish, *b* and *v* should always have the same sound, which is normally similar to *b* as in boy. However, you many occasionally here speakers pronounce it like an English v. Even so, use and listen for a *b* sound. (*vaca*)

x – normally like an English *x* (*taxi*), occasionally like an *s*

y – when followed by a vowel, the same as *ll*, i.e. like the *s* of *measure* (*yo, vaya*)

z – in Latin American Spanish (including Argentine Spanish), the *z* is pronounced exactly like the letter *s* (i.e. like the *ss* of *class* and **never** like the *s* of *nose*)

Accent and Syllable Stress

1) If a word has an written accent, you will always stress that syllable. (*éxito*, *perdí*, *Perú*).

2) If a word does not have a written accent mark and ends with a vowel or the consonants *n* or *s*, then you will stress the second to last syllable (**ha**blo, **ha**blas, **ha**blan).

3) If a word does not have a written accent mark and ends with any consonant other than *n* o *s*, then you will stress the last syllable (regu**lar**, nor**mal**).

Pronouns and Articles

Subject Pronouns
yo – I
vos* – you - familiar (friends, family, people younger than you)
usted (Ud.) – you – formal (strangers, people older than you)

él – he
ella – she

nosotros - we (m.)
nosotras – we (f.)

ustedes (Uds.) – you all**

ellos – they (m.)
ellas – they (f.)

Object Pronouns
me/mí – me
te/ti/vos – you (familiar)
lo/le – him, to him, you, to you (m.-formal)
la/le – her, to her, you, to you (f.-formal)
nos – us, to us
les/los/las – you all, to you all; them, to them

*tú in standard Spanish including in countries like Spain and Mexico
**Please note that the distinction between *you* familiar (vos) and *you* formal (usted) is only observed when speaking to one person. When speaking to more than one personal you will use *ustedes* (Uds.) regardless of who you're speaking to.

Indefinite Articles

un* – a/an (m.)
una – a/an (f.)
unos – some, a few (m.)
unas – some, a few (f.)

un libro – a book
unos libros – some books
una mochila – a bookbag
unas mochilas – some bookbags

Definite Articles

el* – the (m. singular)
la – the (f. singualr)
los – the (m. plural)
las – the (f. plural)

el lápiz – the pencil
los lápices – the pencils
la clase – the class
las clases – the classes

*Feminine singular nouns such *aula* which begin with the vowel *a* and whose pronunciation stress is on the first syllable will be proceeded by the masculine articles *un* (a/an) and *el* (the) rather than the corresponding feminine articles *una* and *la*. Another example of this is the word *agua* (water). This does **not** occur with words such as *alfombra* (carpet) whose pronunciation stress does not fall on the first syllable.

En casa, en clase y en el trabajo
(at home, in class and at work)

La gente (people)
el **padre** – the father
la **madre** – the mother
el **bebé** – the baby
la **beba** – the baby (f.)
el **nene** – the child (m.)
la **nena** – the child (f.)
el **pibe**/la **piba** – the child (informal)
los **nenes/chicos/pibes** – the children
el **chico/muchacho/pibe** – the boy
la **chica/muchacha/piba** – the girl
el **hombre** – the man
la **mujer** – the woman
el **maestro**/la **maestra** – the teacher (grade school)
el **profesor**/la **profesora** – the teacher (in general)
el **alumno**/la **alumna** – the student, pupil (m. & f.)
el **estudiante**/la **estudiante** – the student (m. & f.)

La casa (the house/home)
el **baño** – the bathroom
el **bidé/bidet** – the bidet
el **cajón** – the drawer
el **celular** – the cellphone, mobile phone
el **comedor** – the dining room
el **cuarto**/la **pieza** – the room
el **equipo de música**– the stereo
el **felpudo** – the doormat
el **inodoro** – the toilet
el **living** – the living room
el **muro** – the wall (outside a house or building)
el **pasillo** – the hall/corridor
el **picaporte** – the door handle

el **piso** – the floor
el **placard** – the closet (US)/wardrobe (UK)
el **pomo**/la **perilla** – the doorknob
el **sofá** – the sofa, couch
el **teléfono** – the telephone
el **televisor** – the television (set)
el **timbre** – the bell, doorbell
el **velador** – the lamp

la **alfombra**/el **felpudo** – the bathmat
la **bacha** –the bathroom sink, washbasin
la **bañera** – the bathtub
la **cómoda** – the dresser, chest of drawers
la **colcha** – the bedspread, eiderdown
la **computadora** – the computer
la **cocina** – the kitchen
la **escalera** – the stairs
la **frasada** – the blanket
la **impresora** – the printer
la **luz** – the light, electricity
la **manija** – the door handle
la **mesa** – the table
la **mesita de luz** – night table, bedside table
la **pared** – the wall (inside a house or building)
la **pieza/habitación** – the bedroom
la **puerta** – the door
la **silla** – the chair
la **ventana** – the window

En el trabajo (at work)

el *ascensor* – the elevator/lift
el *edificio* – the building
el *despacho* – the office
el *empleado* – the employee (m.)
el *estudio* – the studio/study
el *jefe* – the boss (m.)

la *empleada* – the employee (f.)
la *entrada* – the entrance
la *jefa* – the boss (f.)
la *oficina* – the office
la *salida* – the exit, way out

Profesiones
abogado – lawyer
actor – actor
actriz – actress
azafata – airline stewardess
bailarín – dancer
bombero - firefighter
cantante - singer
carnicero – butcher
carpintero – carpenter
cartero – mailman/postman
científico - scientist
cocinero – cook
contador público – accountant
dentista – dentist
doctor – doctor
enfermero – nurse
escritor - writer
gaucho – Argentine cowboy

gerente - manager
ingeniero - engineer
médico – doctor/physician
militar – serviceman
ministro – minister
moza/señora/señorita* – waitress
mozo/señor/caballero* – waiter
músico - musician
panadero – baker
pastor – shepherd, pastor
piloto – pilot
plomero – plumber
policía – policeman
político – politician
profesor – teacher
sacerdote – priest
secretario – secretary
soldado – soldier

*Apparently, it is better to address a waiter as *señor* or *caballero* and a waitress as *señora* or *señorita* when speaking to them directly. That is to say that *mozo* and *moza* are probably best used when speaking about waiters and waitresses in third person rather than directly.

En clase
(in class)

tener – to have
(yo) **tengo** – I have
(vos) **tenés** – you have (familiar)
(Ud.) **tiene** – you have (formal)
(él) **tiene** – he has
(ella) **tiene** – she has
(nosotros/nosotras) **tenemos** – we have
(Uds.) **tienen** - you all have
(ellos/ellas) **tienen** – they have

necesitar* – to need
(yo) **necesito** – I need
(vos) **necesitás** – you need (familiar)
(usted) **necesita** – you need (formal)
(él/ella) **necesita** – he/she needs
(nosotros) **necesitamos** – we need
(ustedes) **necesitan** – you all need
(ellos/ellas) **necesitan** – they need

Tengo un libro. – I have a book.
No tengo un libro. – I don't have a book.
Necesito el libro. – I need the book.
No necesito el libro. – I don't need the book.
Hay un libro. – There's a book.
No hay ningún libro. – There isn't any book.
Hay muchos libros. – There are many books.
No hay muchos libros. – There aren't many books.

*The verb **precisar** also means more or less the same thing and contains the same forms, i.e. *preciso, precisás, precisa, precisamos, precisan.*

14

el **asiento** – the seat
tomar asiento – to have/take a seat
el **bloc de hojas** – the notepad
el **borrador** – the eraser/rubber
el **cuaderno** – the notebook
el **ejercicio** – the exercise
el **error** – the error, mistake
el **escritorio** – the desk
el **estante**/la **estantería** – the shelf, bookshelf, shelves
el **examen**/la **prueba** – the exam, test, quiz
el **lápiz** – the pencil
el **libro** – the book
el **marcador** – the marker
el **pizarrón** – the board, chalkboard, blackboard
el **pupitre** – the student desk
el **sacapuntas** – the pencil sharpener
los **apuntes** – notes   *tomar apuntes* – to take notes
el **aula** - the classroom
la **birome/lapicera** – the pen
la **calculadora** – the calculator
la **carpeta** – the folder
la **clase** – the class
la **computadora** – the computer
la **falta** – the spelling mistake, typo, etc.
la **goma (de borrar)** – the rubber eraser
la **hoja de papel** – the piece of paper
la **impresora** – the printer
la **lección** – the lesson
la **libreta** – the notebook, writing book
la **mesa** – the table
la **mochila** – the bookbag, schoolbag, rucksack
la **regla** – the ruler
la **silla** – the chair
la **tijera** – the scissors

Saludos y despedidas
(greetings and farewells)

¡Hola! - Hi!/Hello!
Buen día. – Good morning./Good day.
Buenos días. – Good morning.
Buenas tardes. – Good afternoon.
Buenas noches. – Good evening./Good night.
Adiós. – Good-bye.
Chau./Bai./Salud. – Bye!
Hasta luego./Chau. – See you later.
Hasta pronto. – See you soon.
Hasta mañana. – See you tomorrow.

(el)* Sr. López – Mr. Lopez (Sr.=señor)
(la)* Sra. López – Mrs. Lopez (Sra. = señora)
(la)* Srta. López - Miss (Srta. = señorita)

(el)* Dr. Moreno – Dr. Moreno (m.)
(la)* Dra. Moreno – Dr. Moreno (f.)

*One must use the definite articles *el* and *la* when you are speaking to about these people in third person and not directly to them. For example:

El Sr. López es mi profesor de castellano. – Mr. Lopez is my Spanish teacher.
¡Sr. López! ¿Cómo está usted? – Mr. Lopez! How are you?

señor – sir, Mr.
señora – ma'am, madam, Mrs.
señorita – miss, Miss

¿Cómo estás? – How are you? (familiar)
¿Qué tal? – How's it going?/What's up?

¿Cómo te va? – How's it going?
¿Todo bien? – Is everything okay?
¿Cómo está usted? – How are you? (formal)
¿Cómo están ustedes? – How are you all?

Bien, ¿y vos? – Fine, and you? (familiar)
Bien, ¿y usted? – Fine, and you? (formal)
Bien, ¿y ustedes? – Fine, and you all?

Muy bien. – Very well.
Muy bien, gracias. – Very well, thanks.
Regular. – Okay./So-so.
Mal. – Bad./Not well.

Yo también. – Me too.
Yo tampoco. – Me neither.

Perdone./Disculpe. – Excuse me./Sorry. (formal)

Lo siento. – I'm sorry.
Lo siento mucho. – I'm very sorry.

¿Cómo? – What?/Excuse me? (when you don't understand what someone said)

Gracias. – Thank you./Thanks.
Muchas gracias. – Thank you very much./Thanks a lot.

De nada. – You're welcome.

Por favor. - Please.

¡Bienvenido(s)!/¡Bienvenida(s)! – Welcome!
¡Salud! – Cheers! (with toast)/Bless you! (with sneeze)
Sí. – Yes.
No. – No.
Quizás/Tal vez. – Perhaps./Maybe.
Con mucho gusto. – Gladly.
¡Claro!/¡Claro que sí! – Of course!/Yes, of course!
¡Por supuesto!/¡Cómo no!/¡Desde luego! – Of course./Certainly.

hombre – man
tipo/chabón – man (informal, slang)
cabrón – jerk, rascal, bastard (vulgar)
¡Che!/¡Boludo! – informal words used to address someone, esp. a man; these should only be used with friends or people you know well and not in formal situations, the term "boludo" (literally "big ball") can sometimes mean *idiot* or *fool* in other contexts.
¡Dale! – a very commonly used phrase in Argentina; loosely the equivalent of *¡Ándale!* in Mexican Spanish and *¡Vale!* in Spain; depending on the context it can mean: *okay, go ahead, hurry up, wow, well I'll be!*, etc.

¡Oye!/¡Che! – Hey! (familiar)*
¡Oiga! – Hey! (formal)
¡Oigan! – Hey! (plural)
¿Viste? – You know?/Understand?/You see? (lit. *Did you see?*)
¡Mirá vos! – Wow!/Well, I'll be!/Looky here!

---

*This means "Hey!" when used to attract someone's attention, but it's not normally used as a greeting (that would be "Hola!")

Hablar de vos
(talking about yourself)

¿Quién sos (vos)? – Who are you? (familiar)
¿Quién es (usted)? – Who are you? (formal)
Soy estudiante. – I'm a student.
No soy estudiante. – I'm not a student.
Soy casado/casada. – I'm married.
Soy soltero/soltera. – I'm single.
Tengo un hijo. – I have a son./I have one son.
Tengo una hija. – I have a daughter./I have one daughter.
Tengo tres hijos. – I have three sons./I have three children.
Tengo cuatro hijas. – I have four daughters.
Tengo un hermanito. – I have a little brother.
Tengo una hermanita. – I have a younger sister.
Tengo un perro y dos gatos. – I have a dog and two cats.
Soy argentino/argentina. – I'm Argentine./I'm Argentinean.
Soy estadounidense/norteamericano(a). – I'm American.
Soy canadiense. – I'm Canadian.
Soy italiano/italiana. – I'm Italian.
Soy inglés/inglesa. – I'm English.
Soy español/española. – I'm Spanish.
Soy mejicano/mejicana. – I'm Mexican.
Soy alemán/alemana. – I'm German.
Soy francés/francesa. – I'm French.
Soy irlandés/irlandesa. – I'm Irish.
Soy chino/china. – I'm Chinese.
Soy japonés/japonesa. – I'm Japanese.
Soy coreano/coreana. – I'm Korean.
Soy ruso/rusa. – I'm Russian.
Soy polaco/polaca. – I'm Polish.
Soy australiano/australiana. – I'm Australian.
Soy brasileiro/brasileira. – I'm Brazilian. (**not**
brasileño/brasileña)

poder (can, to be able)

puedo – I can, I'm able
podés – you can (familiar)
puede – he/she can; you can (formal)
podemos – we can
pueden – they can, you all can

¿Podés hablar castellano? – Can you speak Spanish? (most common)*
¿Podés hablar español? – Can you speak Spanish? (less common)*
Sólo hablo un poco. – I only speak a little.
No, no hablo castellano. – No, I don't speak Spanish.
No, pero hablo italiano. – No, but I speak Italian.
¿Hablás inglés? – Do you speak English? (familiar)
¿Habla usted inglés? – Do you speak English? (formal)
¿Hablan ustedes inglés? – Do you all speak English?
Sí, lo hablamos. – Yes, we speak it.
No, no lo hablamos. - No, we don't speak it.

Los idiomas del mundo
(languages of the world)
alemán – German
chino – Chinese
coreano – Korean
francés - French
japonés – Japanese
holandés/neerlandés – Dutch
italiano – Italian
polaco - Polish
portugués – Portuguese
ruso – Russian

*Most Argentines prefer to refer to Spanish as *castellano*.

20

¿Dónde vivís (vos)? – Where do you live? (familiar)
¿Dónde vive (Ud.)? – Where do you live? (formal)
Vivo... – I live...
No vivo... – I'don't live...
Vivimos... – We live...
No vivimos... – We don't live...

en **Bruselas.** – in Brussels.
en la **Cuidad de Méjico.** – in Mexico City.
en **Florencia.** – in Florence.
en **Ginebra.** – in Geneva.
en la **Habana.** – in Havana.
en la **Haya.** – in the Hague.
en **Lisboa.** – in Lisbon.
en **Londres.** – in London.
en **Marsella**. – in Marseille.
en **Moscú**. – in Moscow.
en **Nápoles.** – in Naples.
en **Nueva York.** – in New York.
en **París.** – in Paris.
en **Praga** – in Prague.
en **Roma**. – in Rome.
en **Viena**. – in Vienna.
en **Venecia**. – in Venice.

en la calle Nacional, 10 – in 10 National Street
en la avenida Constitución, 25 – in 25 Constitution
Avenue
en el campo - in the country (i.e. outside the city)
en el centro – downtown/in the city center
en la ciudad – in the city/in town
en las afueras/en las provincias – in the suburbs

Las presentaciones
(introductions)

¿Cómo te llamás (vos)? – What's your name? (familiar)
¿Cómo se llama (usted)? – What's your name? (formal)
Me llamo... – My name's...
Mi nombre es... – My name is...
(Yo) soy... – I'm...

Te presento a... – I'd like you to meet... (familiar)
Le presento a... – I'd like you to meet...(formal)
Les presento a... – I'd like you all to meet...

Mucho gusto. – Nice to meet you.
Mucho gusto en conocerte. – It's very nice to meet you. (familiar)
Mucho gusto en conocerle/conocerlo. – It's very nice to meet you. (m.- formal)
Mucho gusto en conocerle/conocerla. – It's very nice to meet you. (f. - formal)
Encantado. - Delighted. (male speaker)
Encantada. - Delighted. (female speaker)

Igualmente. – Likewise./Same here.
Un placer. – A pleasure./It's been a pleasure.
El gusto es mío. – The pleasure was mine.

Éste es mi amigo... – This is my friend...(m.)
Ésta es mi amiga... – This is my friend...(f.)

Éstos son mis amigos... – These are my friends...(m. or mixed)
Éstas son mis amigas... – These are my friends...(all females)

mi compañero/mi compañera – my classmate, mate, colleage, co-worker

mi novio – my boyfriend
mi novia – my girlfriend

mi marido/esposo – my husband/spouse
mi mujer/esposa – my wife/spouse

mi padre – my father
mi papá – my dad

mi madre – my mother
mi mamá – my mom/mum

mis padres/mis papás – my parents
mi hermano – my brother
mi hermana – my sister

mi hijo – my son
mi hija – my daughter

mi tío – my uncle
mi tía – my aunt

mi abuelo – my grandfather
mi abuela - my grandmother

mi primo/prima – my cousin

Countries and Languages
(see also page 20)

¿**De dónde sos?** – Where are you from? (familiar)
¿**De dónde es usted?** – Where are you from? (formal)
Soy... – I'm...
¿**De dónde son ustedes?** – Where are you all from?
Somos... – We're...

de Méjico – from Mexico.
de (los) Estados Unidos. – from the U.S..
de la Gran Bretaña. – from Great Britain.
de Irlanda. – from Ireland.
de Italia. – from Italy.
de Suiza. – from Switzerland.
de Francia. – from France.
de Alemania. – from Germany.
de España. – from Spain.
de Japón./del Japón. – from Japan.
de China./de la China. – from China.
de (la) Argentina – from Argentina (remember that the *g* is pronounced like an *h*!)

¿**Podés hablar castellano?** – Can you speak Spanish? (most common)
¿**Podés hablar español?** – Can you speak Spanish? (less common)
Sólo hablo un poco. – I only speak a little.
No, no hablo castellano. – No, I don't speak Spanish.
No, pero hablo italiano. – No, but I speak Italian.
¿**Hablás inglés?** – Do you speak English? (familiar)
¿**Habla usted inglés?** – Do you speak English? (formal)
¿**Hablan ustedes inglés?** – Do you all speak English?
Sí, lo hablamos. – Yes, we speak it.
No, no lo hablamos. - No, we don't speak it.

Los idiomas del mundo
(languages of the world)
alemán – German
chino – Chinese
coreano – Korean
francés - French
japonés – Japanese
holandés/neerlandés – Dutch
italiano – Italian
polaco - Polish
portugués – Portuguese
ruso – Russian

24

Describir la ropa y a la gente
(describing clothing and people)

ser (to be)
(yo) **soy** – I am
(vos) **sos*** – you are (familiar)
(Ud.) **es** – you are (formal)**
(él) **es** – he is
(ella) **es** – she is
(nosotros/nosotras) **somos** – we are
(Uds.) **son** – you all are**
(ellos/ellas) **son** – they are

¿Cómo es él? – What's he like?
¿Cómo es ella? – What's she like?
¿Cómo son ellos? – What are they like? (m.)
¿Cómo son ellas? – What are they like? (f.)
Él es seri**o**. – He's serious.
Ella es seri**a**. – She's serious.
Ellos son seri**os**. – They're serious. (m.)
Ellas son seri**as**. – They're serious. (f.)

alto - tall
bajo – short (in stature)
delgado - thin
flaco – skinny
gordo – fat

*This would be *tú eres* in Standard Spanish.
**Remember that *Ud.* is the abbreviation for *usted*, and *Uds.* is the abbreviation for *ustedes*. You may occasionally see these abbreviations written as *Vd.* and *Vds.* as they were originally *vuestra merced* (your mercy) and *vuestras mercedes* (your mercies) in medieval Spanish.

grande – big/large
pequeño, chico – small

lindo/linda – attractive/good-looking
bonito – pretty
lindo/hermoso - beautiful
feo - ugly

serio – serious
gracioso/chistoso/cómico – funny

divertido – fun, entertaining
interesante – interesting
aburrido – boring, bored

inteligente/listo – intelligent

simpático/amable – nice, kind, friendly
sociable – sociable
antipático – not nice, disagreeable

cortés – polite, courteous
grosero/maleducado - rude

trabajador(a) – hardworking
perezoso – lazy

rubio – blond, fair
castaño – brown-haired
pelirrojo – red-haired

tener – to have

(yo) **tengo** – I have
(vos) **tenés** – you have (familiar)
(Ud.) **tiene** – you have (formal)
(él) **tiene** – he has
(ella) **tiene** – she has

(nosotros/nosotras) **tenemos** – we have
(Uds.) **tienen** - you all have
(ellos/ellas) **tienen** – they have

el pelo largo – long hair
el pelo corto – short hair

el pelo lacio – straight hair
el pelo rizado – curly hair
el pelo ondulado – wavy hair

el pelo negro – black hair
el pelo castaño – brown hair
el pelo pelirrojo – red hair
el pelo rubio – blond hair, fair hair

los ojos marrones – brown eyes
los ojos verdes – green eyes
los ojos azules – blue eyes

usar/llevar (ropa)
to wear (clothes)

(Yo) **uso/llevo**... – I wear...
(Vos) **usás/llevás**... – You wear...(familiar)
(Él/Ella) **usa/lleva**... – He/She wears...

(Nosotros/Nosotras) **usamos/llevamos**... – We wear...
(Ustedes) **usan/llevan**... – You all wear...
(Ellos/Ellas) **usan/llevan**... – They wear...

el **albornoz** – terrycloth bathrobe
el **algodón** – cotton
el **buzo** – sweatshirt
el **calzoncillo/slip** – underpants (for men)
el **cierre** – zip, zipper
el **cinto/cinturón** - belt
el **corpiño** – bra
el **deshabille** – bathrobe, dressing gown
el **hilo** – thread
el **impermeable** – raincoat
el **jogging** – jogging suit, tracksuit
el **pantalón**/los **pantalones** – pants/trousers
el **pañuelo** – handkerchief, decorative scarf
el **paraguas** – umbrella
el **piyama** – pajamas, pyjama
el **saco/abrigo** - coat
el **sobretodo/tapado** – overcoat, trenchcoat
el **sombrero** - hat
el **sweater** – sweater, jumper
el **traje** - suit
el **vestido** – dress
los **anteojos/lentes** – glasses
los **aretes** – earrings
los **can-can** - pantyhose, nylons, tights

los **guantes** - gloves
los **jeans** – jeans
los **soquetes** – small socks, short socks
los **tacos** - heels
los **zapatos** – shoes

la **blusa** – blouse
la(s) **bombacha(s)** – panties, knickers
la **bufanda** – winter scarf
la **camisa** – shirt
la **cartera** - handbag
la **chalina** – female scarf, foulard
la **chaqueta/campera** - jacket
la **corbata** – tie
la **lana** – wool
la **lencería** – lingerie
la **malla** – bathing suit, swim suit
la **polera** – turtleneck shirt or sweater
la **pollera** – skirt
la **remera** – T-shirt
la **seda** – silk
las **botas** – boots
las **calzas** – tights, leotards
las **medias** – socks
las **ojotas** – flip-flops
las **sandalias** – sandals

Los colores
(colors)

blanco – white
negro – black
marrón – brown
marrón claro – light brown, tan, khaki
rojo – red
rosa/rosado – pink
violeta – purple
lila – light purple
bordeaux – burgundy (pronounced *bordó*)
naranja/anaranjado – orange
amarillo – yellow
azul – blue
azul marino – dark blue, navy blue
celeste – light blue/sky blue
verde – green
gris – gray/grey

Los números, las fechas y hablar de la hora
(numbers, dates and telling time)

cero - 0
uno - 1
dos - 2
tres - 3
cuatro - 4
cinco - 5
seis - 6
siete - 7
ocho - 8
nueve - 9
diez - 10
once - 11
doce - 12
trece - 13
catorce - 14
quince - 15
dieciséis - 16
diecisiete - 17
dieciocho - 18
diecinueve - 19
veinte - 20
veintiuno - 21
veintidós - 22
veintitrés - 23
veinticuatro - 24
veinticinco - 25
veintiséis - 26
veintisiete - 27
veintiocho - 28
veintinueve - 29

treinta - 30
treinta y uno - 31
treinta y dos - 32
treinta y tres - 33, etc.

cuarenta - 40
cincuenta - 50
sesenta - 60
setenta - 70
ochenta - 80
noventa - 90

cien - 100
ciento uno - 101
ciento dos - 102
ciento tres - 103
ciento cuatro - 104
ciento cinco - 105, etc.
doscientos - 200
trescientos - 300
cuatrocientos - 400
quinientos - 500
seiscientos - 600
setecientos - 700
ochocientos - 800
novecientos – 900

mil – 1.000
dos mil – 2.000
diez mil – 10.000
un millón – 1.000.000
dos millones – 2.000.000

¿Qué hora es? – What time is it?

Es la... – It's...

Son las... – It's... (for numbers higher than one)

Es la una. – It's one o'clock.

Es la una en punto. – It's one o'clock on the dot.

Es la una y cinco. – It's 1:05.

Es la una y diez. – It's 1:10.

Es la una y cuarto. – It's 1:15./It's quarter past one.

Es la una y veinticinco. – It's 1:25.

Es la una y media. – It's 1:30./It's half past one.

Son las dos menos veinticinco. (1:35)

Son las dos menos veinte. (1:40)

Son las dos menos cuarto. (1:45)

Son las dos menos diez. (1:50)

Son las dos. – It's two o'clock.

Son las tres. – It's three o'clock.

¿A qué hora...? – At what time...?

A la una. – At one o'clock.

A las tres. – At three o'clock.

de la mañana – in the morning

de la tarde – in the afternoon

de la noche – in the evening

al mediodía – at noon/midday

a la medianoche –at midnight

esta mañana – this morning

esta tarde – this afternoon

esta noche – this evening/tonight

anoche – last night

To tell time in the past, you'll use the imperfect past verb forms *era* and *eran* instead of the present forms *es* and *son*. For example:

Era la **una.** – It was one o'clock.

Eran las **tres.** – It was three o'clock.

33

Los días de la semana
(the days of the week)

lunes - Monday
martes - Tuesday
miércoles - Wednesday
jueves - Thursday
viernes - Friday
sábado - Saturday
domingo – Sunday

Los meses del año
(the months of the year)

enero - January
febrero - February
marzo - March
abril - April
mayo - May
junio - June
julio - July
agosto - August
septiembre - September
octubre - October
noviembre - November
diciembre - December

Las estaciones del año
(the seasons of the year)

el invierno - winter
la primavera - spring
el verano - summer
el otoño – autumn/fall

¿Qué día es hoy? – What day is today?
Hoy es lunes. – Today's Monday.
¿Cuál es la fecha de hoy? – What's the date today?
Hoy es el... – Today's the...
Hoy es el cinco de marzo. – Today's March 5th.
5 de abril de 2005 – March 5, 2005

hoy – today
ayer – yesterday
anteayer – the day before yesterday
mañana – tomorrow
pasado mañana – the day after tomorrow

esta semana – this week
la semana que viene – next week*
la semana pasada – last week

este mes – this month
el mes que viene – next month*
el mes pasado – last month

este año – this year
el año que viene – next year*
el año pasado – last year

Please note: In Spanish, cardinal numbers are used for dates, and not ordinal numbers as in English. The only exception is the first of the month which is sometimes called *el primero* instead of *el uno*.

*or *la próxima semana, el próximo mes, el próximo año*

Las actividades y los lugares
(activities and places)

(a mí) **me gusta(n)** – I like
(a vos**) te gusta(n)** – you like (familiar)
(a él) **le gusta(n)** – he likes
(a ella) **le gusta(n)** – she likes
(a usted) **le gusta(n)** – you like (formal)
(a nosotros/nosotras) **nos gusta(n)** – we like
(a ustedes) **les gusta(n)** – you all like
(a ellos/ellas) **les gusta(n)** – they like

Me **gusta** el fútbol. – I like football/soccer. (singular)
Me **gustan** los pibes. – I like children. (plural)

andar/caminar – to walk
bailar – to dance
cantar – to sing
cocinar – to cook
correr – to run
dar un paseo – to go for a stroll/walk
dibujar – to draw
dormir – to sleep
escuchar música – to listen to music
esquiar – to ski
hacer ejercicio – to exercise, work out
ir al cine – to go the movies/cinema
ir a los conciertos – to go to concerts
ir de compras – to go shopping
jugar al fútbol – to play soccer/football
leer – to read
nadar – to swim
patinar – to skate
pintar – to paint
tocar la guitarra/el piano – to play the guitar/piano
viajar – to travel

The Verb *ir* (to go)

¿Adónde vas?/¿Adónde va usted? – <small>Where are you going?</small>
Voy... – I'm going...

¿Adónde va él/ella? – Where is he/she going?
Él/Ella va... – He/She is going...

¿Adónde van Uds.? – Where are you all going?
Vamos... – We're going...

¿Adónde van ellos/ellas? – Where are they going?
Ellos/Ellas van... – They're going...

a + el = al
al aeropuerto – to the airport
al bar – to the bar
al baile – to the dance
al boliche – to the bar/club/disco
al bosque – to the forest
al café – to the café
al campo - to the country(side)
al centro – downtown/to the city center
al cine – to the cinema/movie theater
al concierto – to the concert
al estadio – to the stadium
al gimnasio – to the gym
al gran almacén – to the department store
al hotel – to the hotel
al hospital – to the hospital
al juego/al partido – to the game/match
al lago – to the lake

*Often pronounced as if it were spelled *restaurán*.

al mercado – to the market
al museo – to the museum
al parque – to the park
al partido/a la partida – to the match
al restaurant(e)* – to the restaurant
al shopping – to the shopping center
al supermercado – to the supermarket

a la biblioteca – to the library
a la carnicería – to the butcher shop
a casa - home
a la casa – to the house
a la escuela – to (the) school
a la estación – to the station
a la farmacia – to the pharmacy/chemist's
a la fiambrería – to the deli, sausage and cheese shop
a la heladería – to the icecream shop/parlor
a la librería – to the bookstore/shop
a la iglesia – to the church
a la misa – to (the) mass
a las montañas – to the mountains
a la panadería – to the bakery, bread shop
a la pastelería – to the pastry shop
a la pescadería – to the fishmonger, fish shop
a la piscina/a la pileta – to the swimming pool
a la playa/al mar – to the beach/sea
a la plaza – to the square
a la tienda – to the store/shop
a la tienda de ropa – to the clothing store/shop
a la universidad – to the university

¿Dónde estás?/¿Dónde está Ud.? – Where are you?
Estoy... – I am...
¿Dónde está él/ella? – Where is he/she?
Está... – He/She is...
¿Dónde están Uds.? – Where are you all?
Estamos... – We are...
¿Dónde están ellos/ellas? – Where are they?
Están... – They are...

en el aeropuerto – at the airport
en el banco – at the bank
en el centro – downtown/in the city center
en el restaurante – at the restaurant
en la oficina/en el despacho – at the office

Pedir indicaciones
(asking for directions)

¿Dónde está...? – Where is...?
¿Dónde están...? – Where are...?
¿Puede usted decirme dónde está...? – Can you tell me where is...?

Vaya.... - Go...
Doble... - Turn...
Siga.../Continue - Continue...
a/hasta – to/until
de/desde - from
derecho/recto - straight
a la derecha – right/to the right
a la izquierda – left/to the left

una cuadra – one block
dos cuadras – two blocks
(al) norte - north
(al) sur - south
(al) este - east
(al) oeste - west

el **camino** – the way, route
el **semáforo** –the traffic light
la **avenida** – the avenue
la **calle** – the street
la **dirección** – the direction or address
la **esquina** – the corner
la **vereda** – the sidewalk

aquí/acá – here/over here
allí - there
allá – there/over there

encima (de) – on top (of)
debajo (de) – below/underneath

arriba (de) - above
abajo/por debajo - below

adentro/dentro de - inside
afuera/fuera de - outside

cerca (de) – near, close to
lejos (de) – far (from)
delante (de) - in front (of)
detrás (de) - behind

adelante/por delante - ahead
atrás/por detrás – behind

ir (to go)
voy – I go, I'm going
vas – you go, you're going
va – he goes/he's going
vamos – we go, we're going
van – they go, you all go

venir (to come)
vengo – I come, I'm coming
venís – you come, you're coming
viene – he comes, he's coming
venimos – we come, we're coming
vienen – they come, you all come

Modes of Transport

andar/caminar – to walk, to go by foot
viajar – to travel

a pie – on foot
a caballo – by horse

en auto – by car
en autobús – by bus*
en avión – by plane
en barco – by boat
en bicicleta - bike
en camión – by truck, lorry
en moto – by motorcycle
en subte – by subway/underground
en tranvía – by tram, trolley, streetcar
en tren – by train

*also *en colectivo* or *en ómnibus*

Hablar del tiempo
(talking about the weather)

hacer (to do, make)
hago – I do, make
hacés – you do, make
hace – he does/she does/it does
hacemos – we do, make
hacen – they do, make/you all do, make

¿Qué tiempo hace? – How's the weather?
Hace buen tiempo. – It's nice.
Hace mal tiempo. – It's nasty.
Hace frío. – It's cold.
Hace mucho frío. – It's very cold.
Hace calor. – It's hot.
Hace mucho calor. – It's very hot.
Hace fresco. – It's cool.
Está nublado. – It's cloudy.
Hay sol. – It's sunny.
Hay viento. – It's windy.

la lluvia - rain
llover – to rain
Llueve.... - It rains...
Está lloviendo. – It's raining.
la nieve - snow
nevar – to snow
Nieva... – It snows...
Está nevando. – It's snowing.
el trueno - thunder
tronar – to thunder
Truena.../Hay trueno... – There's thunder...
Está tronando... – It's thundering.
Hay relámpago(s). – There's lightning.

43

El cuerpo humano
(the human body)

la **cabeza** - head
la *frente* - forehead
el *cráneo* - skull
el *cerebro* – brain
la *oreja*/el *oído* – ear (outer & inner)
el *pelo*/el *cabello* - hair

la **cara**/el **rostro** - face
el *ojo* - eye
la *mejilla* - cheek
la *nariz* - nose

la **boca** - mouth
el *labio* - lip
la *lengua* - tongue
el *diente* - tooth

la **mandíbula** - jaw
el **mentón** - chin

el **cuello** - neck
la **garganta** - throat

la **espalda** - back

el **brazo** - arm
el *hombro* - shoulder
el *codo* - elbow
la *muñeca* - wrist

la **mano** - hand
el *nudillo* - knuckle
el *dedo* - finger
la *uña* - fingernail

el **pecho** - chest
la *costilla* - rib
el *corazón* - heart
el *pulmón* - lung
el *hígado* – liver
el *riñón* - kidney

el **estómago** - stomach
el *ombligo* - navel

la **pierna/gamba** - leg
la *rodilla* - knee

el **pie** – foot
el **dedo del pie** - toe

la **piel** - skin

la **sangre** - blood

La comida, las bebidas y la cocina
(food, drinks and the kitchen)

El desayuno (breakfast)
el *cereal* – cereal
el *dulce de leche* – a caramel-like spread extremely popular in Argentina, often spread on toast, but also used in cakes and pastries, etc.
el *pan* – bread
el *panecillo* – breadroll
el *pancito de manteca* – breadroll in some cases similar to an American biscuit or a British scone
la *factura* – sweetroll, bun, pastry
la *figaz(z)a de manteca* – similar to *pancito de manteca*
la *jalea* – jelly/jam
la *manteca* – butter
la *media luna* – croissant (lit. half-moon)
la *mermelada* – jam
la *tostada* – toast
las *masitas* – cookies, biscuits

El almuerzo (lunch)
el *sandwich/sangüiche* – sandwich
el *pancho* – hotdog
la *empanada* – pastry filled with meat and/or vegetables, similar to pasties in U.K.
la *ensalada* – salad
la *hamburguesa* – hamburger
las *milanesas* – fried breaded meat fillets
las *papas fritas* – french fries, chips
la *sopa* – soup
la *cena* – dinner, supper
la *merienda* – snack, light meal

Las bebidas (drinks)

el *agua* - water

el *jugo* - juice

la *leche* - milk

la *limonada* - lemonade

el *café* - coffee

el *té* – tea

el *mate* – Argentina's national beverage, a type of tea which is drunk from a gourd-like container which is also called *el mate*. The metal straw used to sip it is called *la bombilla* and *mate* is often passed from person to person as matter of custom.

el *hielo* - ice

la *cerveza/birra* - beer

el *vino* - wine

el *aguardiente/coñac* – brandy/cognac

el *whisky* – whisky

La mesa (the table)

el *mantel* – table cloth

los *cubiertos* – flatware, cutlery

el *cuchillo*- knife

el *tenedor* - fork

la *cuchara* - spoon

la *servilleta* – napkin, serviette

el *plato* – plate, dish

la *taza* - cup

el *vaso* - glass

la *jarra* – pitcher/jug

la *sal* - salt

la *pimienta* - pepper

el *azúcar* - sugar

la *mostaza* - mustard

la *mayonesa* – mayonnaise

La fruta (fruit)

el *ananás* – pineapple
el *damasco/albaricoque* – apricot
el *durazno* - peach
el *higo* – fig
el *limón* – lemon
el *melón* - melon
la *banana* – banana
la *cereza* - cherry
la *ciruela* - plum
la *ciruela pasa* - prune
la *frambuesa* - raspberry
la *frutilla* - strawberry
la *manzana* - apple
la *mora* – blackberry
la *naranja* - orange
la *pera* - pear
la *sandía* – watermelon
la *toronja* – grapefruit
la *uva* - grape
la *uva pasa* - raisin

Las verduras (vegetables)

el *ajo* – garlic
el *maíz* – corn, maize
el *pepino* - cucumber
el *pepinillo* – pickle/gherkin
el *repollo* - cabbage
el *tomate* – tomato
los *porotos* - beans
la *aceituna* - olive
la *cebolla* - onion
la *coliflor* – cauliflower
la *espinaca* - spinach
la *lechuga* – lettuce
la *zanahoria* - carrot
las *arvejas* – peas
las *chauchas* – green beans

Las carnes (meats)

el *asado* – grilled meat, barbecue
el *bife* - steak
el *bife asado* – grilled steak
el *cerdo* – pork
el *chorizo* – red sausage
el *cordero* - lamb
el *jamón* – ham
el *jamón crudo* – cured ham
el *jamón cocido* – cooked ham
el *pavo* – turkey
el *pollo* - chicken
la *carne de vaca* – beef
la *morcilla* – blood sausage, black pudding
la *panceta* - bacon

la *salchicha* - sausage
los *fiambres* – cold cuts, sliced meats
las *albondigas* - meatballs
las *milanesas* – fried breaded meat fillets

Los mariscos (seafood)
el *atún* – tuna
el *bacalao* – cod
el *calamar* - squid
el *camarón* - shrimp
el *pescado* – fish
el *pulpo* - octopus
el *salmón* – salmon
la *almeja* - clam
la *anchoa* - anchovy
la *langosta* - lobster
la *ostra* - oyster
la *trucha* - trout

Los postres (desserts)
dulce/caramelo – sweet, candy
dulce de leche – caramel
chocolate - chocolate
torta/pastelito - cake, pie/pastry
helado – ice cream

Misceláneo (miscellaneous)

horneado - baked
cocido - cooked
frito - fried
asado – roasted/grilled
sazonado - seasoned
relleno – stuffed

el *aceite* - oil
el *aperitivo* – starter, appetizer
el *arroz* - rice
el *caldo* – broth
el *guisado* - stew
el *maní* - peanut
el *panecillo* – roll, bun
el *pochoclo* – popcorn
el *puré de papas* – mashed potatoes
el *queso* – cheese
la *almendra* – almond
la *crema* - cream
la *galleta* – cookie, biscuit, cracker
la *harina* – flour
la *miel* - honey
la *papa* – potato
la *pasta* - pasta
la *salsa* – sauce, gravy
los *espaguetis* - spaghetti
los *fideos/tallerines* – noodles
los *huevos* - eggs

En la cocina (in the kitchen)

el *balde*/la *cubeta* – pale/bucket
el *cucharón* – ladle, large spoon
el *horno* – oven
el *sacacorchos* – corkscrew
el *trapeador* – mop
la *botella* - bottle
la *cacerola* - saucepan
la *cocina* (eléctrica o de gas) – stove (US)/cooker (UK)
la *copa* – goblet
la *escoba* - broom
la *heladera* – fridge
la *lata* – can/tin
la *olla* - pot
la *sartén* – frying pan

Forming *yes/no* Questions in Spanish

A yes/no question is a question that can be logically answered with either yes or no. Some questions are not yes/no questions. For example, the question *¿Cómo estás?* (How are you?) is not a yes/no question because it cannot be answered logically with either yes or no. An example of a yes/no question would be the question *¿Ella toca el piano?* (Does she play the piano?) because a person would have to answer either "Yes, she plays the piano." or "No, she doesn't play the piano.".

In Spanish, there are three ways to form a yes/no question:

1) Put question marks around a statement and change the tone of your voice to make the statement sound like a question. For example:

Ella toca el piano. (She plays the piano.) This is a statement.

However, "¿Ella toca el piano?" becomes a question when you add question marks and change the tone of your voice.

2) Place the subject after verb, add question marks and change the tone of your voice. For example:

¿Toca ella el piano? or *¿Toca el piano ella?* (The subject is now placed after the verb.)

3) Use a statement followed with a comma and any of these three confirmation tags:

(the tone of your voice only changes when you say the confirmation tag)

¿verdad? (truth?)

¿no? (no?)

¿no es cierto?/¿no es verdad? (isn't that so?/isnt' that true?)

Ella toca el piano, ¿verdad? (She plays the piano, doesn't she?)

Ella no toca el piano, ¿verdad? (She doesn't play the piano, does she?)

Ella toca el piano, ¿no?/Ella toca el piano, ¿no es cierto? - (She plays the piano, isn't that right?) – These two options should only be used with affirmative sentences.

53

Answering *yes/no* Questions in Spanish

In English, when the words yes or no begin a sentence, they are generally followed by a comma, for example:

Yes, I speak Spanish.
No, I don't speak Spanish.

Likewise in Spanish, the words sí and no are followed by a comma when they begin a sentence. However, if the word no is *not followed by a comma*, it does not mean *no* as in English but rather *not* or *don't*. For example:

No, no hablo castellano. (No, I don't speak Spanish)

Notice that the first *no* which is followed by a comma means *no* whereas the second *no* which is not followed by a comma means *don't*. Be careful not to place a comma after the word *no* when it means *don't* because you should only place a comma after it when it means *no* as in English. Using an unnecessary comma can change the meaning of the whole sentence! Look at the following two examples:

No hablo castellano. (I don't speak Spanish.)
No, hablo castellano. (No, I speak Spanish.)

If someone asked you, "¿Estudiás castellano?" (Do you study Spanish?), you could either answer:

Sí, estudio castellano. (Yes, I study Spanish.)
or you could answer:
No, no estudio castellano. (No, I don't study Spanish.)

or you could answer:

No, estudio francés. (No, I study French.)

Interrogative vs. Yes/No Questions in Spanish

In Spanish, as well as in English, there are two types of questions: *Yes/No questions* which can be logically answered with either yes or no and *interrogative questions* which cannot be logically answered with either yes or no. For example, the question "Are you a teacher?" is a yes/no question because it can be logically answered with either yes or no. However, the question "Why do you like being a teacher?" is an interrogative question and not a yes/no question because it cannot be logically answered with either yes or no.

There are three ways to form a yes/no question in Spanish:

1) Put question marks around a statement and change the tone of your voice to make it sound like a question. For example: *¿Él es maestro?* (He's a teacher?)

2) Put question marks, place the subject after the verb and change the tone of your voice to make it sound like a question. For example: *¿Es él maestro?* or *¿Es maestro él?*

3) Put a comma at the end of a statement with a confirmation tag surrounded by question marks. The tone of your voice only changes with the confirmation tag. For example:
Es maestro, ¿verdad? or *Es maestro, ¿no?* or *Es maestro, ¿no es cierto?*
Notice that with yes/no questions the word order is flexible, that is to say that either the subject or the verb may come first.

However, with interrogative questions, *the verb normally comes first*. For example:

¿Cómo está Ud.? - How are you? (formal)
¿Dónde está Miguel? - Where is Miguel?
¿Cuántos lápices tiene ella? - How many pencils does she have?

Remember that an interrogative question will always contain one of the following interrogative words or phrases:

cómo - how? (also what?)
qué - what? (also which?)
por qué - why?
cuál/cuáles - which? (also what?)
cuándo - when?

cuánto/cuánta - how much?
cuántos/cuántas - how many?

dónde - where?
de dónde - from where?
adónde - to where?

quién/quiénes - who?
de quién/de quiénes - of whom?/from whom?/whose?
a quién/a quiénes - to whom?
para quién/para quiénes - for whom?

Notice that all interrogative words have accent marks. This is not for pronunciation purposes but rather to identify them as interrogative words or to distinguish them from the same word used in a non-interrogative fashion. Some words change meanings when used non-interrogatively. For example:

cómo - how?
como - like, as
como - I eat

qué - what?/which?
que - that, than

por qué - why?
porque - because

Also remember that since the pronouns *yo, vos*, nosotros* have distinctive verb forms in most tenses (of these three, only the pronoun *yo* does not have a distinctive form in certain tenses/moods), they will often be omitted in both yes/no and interrogative questions thereby making the word order of the question irrelevant. However, if these pronouns *are* included in an interrogative question, then the verb normally comes first. Sometimes these pronouns will be included in a question for reasons of emphasis. For example:

¿Dónde trabajo *yo*? - Where do *I* work? (you are repeating the question)

¿Dónde trabajás *vos*?* - Where do *you* work? (more emphasis on the pronoun "vos")

57

¿Dónde trabajamos *nosotros*? - Where do *we* work? (you are repeating the question)

The English verb forms *do*, *does* and *did* are frequently used in questions; however, such words are not used to form questions in Spanish and therefore do not translate into Spanish. For example:

Do you speak Spanish? - *¿Hablás castellano?* (literally: You speak Spanish?)
Does he speak Spanish? - *¿Él habla castellano?* (literally: He speaks Spanish?)
What did you say? - *¿Qué dijiste?* (literally: What you said?)
Where did they go? - *¿Adónde fueron ellos?* (literally: [To] where they went?)

*This is the pronoun *tú* in Standard Spanish.

The English verb forms *do*, *does* and *did* are also used to make a sentence negative in English which is also **not** the case in Spanish. For example:

I do not speak Spanish. - *No hablo español.* (literally: I no speak Spanish.)

He does not speak Spanish. - *Él no habla español.* (literally: He no speaks Spanish.)

I did not go to the party. - *No fui a la fiesta.* (literally: I no went to the party.)

Basic Grammar

Regular Verbs in the Present Tense

In Spanish the infinitive form of the verb always ends with the letter *r*. All verbs in Spanish fall into three categories:

1) those whose infinitive ends with –ar
(for example: bail*ar* - to dance)

2) those whose infinitive ends with –er
(for example: corr*er* - to run)

3) those whose infinitive ends with –ir
(for example: viv*ir* - to live)

Verbs in ArgentineSpanish have five forms which correspond to the following pronouns:

1. **yo** (I)
2. **vos*** (you-familiar)
3. **él** (he), **ella** (she), **Ud.** (you-formal)
4. **nosotros/nosotras** (we)
5. **ellos/ellas** (they); **Uds.**(you all)

*tú in Standard Spanish

To conjugate a regular verb in the present tense into its five forms you must first *remove* the –ar, –er or –ir from the infinitive. The part that remains is known as the root or stem:

bailar (bail)
correr (corr)
vivir (viv)

To the stem you add the following endings which correspond to the five forms mentioned above:

<u>AR Verbs</u>: (bailar)
1. – o
2. – ás
3. –a
4. –amos
5. –an

bail*o* - I dance
bail*ás* - you dance
bail*a* - he/she dances, you dance
bail*amos* - we dance
bail*an* - they dance, you all dance

Other regular –ar verbs:

acabar - to finish
acompañar - to accompany
alquilar - to rent
andar - to walk
apagar - to turn off
ayudar - to help
bailar - to dance
buscar - to look for
caminar - to walk
cambiar - to change, exchange
cantar - to sing
cenar - to have dinner/supper
cocinar - to cook
comprar - to buy
contestar - to answer
cruzar - to cross
cuidar - to take care of
dejar - to let, leave behind
descansar - to rest
desayunar - to have breakfast
doblar - to turn, fold
enseñar - to teach, show
entrar - to enter, go in
escuchar - to listen, hear
esperar - to hope, wait
estudiar - to study
ganar - to win, earn
hablar - to speak, talk
invitar - to invite

lavar - to wash
levantar - to lift
limpiar - to clean
llamar - to call
llegar - to arrive
llevar - to carry, wear
mandar - to send
manejar – to manage, drive
mirar - to watch, look at
nadar - to swim
necesitar - to need
olvidar - to forget
ordenar - to arrange, put in order
pagar - to pay (for)
pasar - to happen, pass
pasear - to go for a walk
patinar - to skate
pintar - to paint
planchar - to iron
practicar - to practice
preparar - to prepare
quedar - to be (located)
quitar - to take away
regatear - to bargain
sacar - to get, take, take out
terminar - to finish, end
tocar - to play music
tomar - to take, drink
trabajar - to work
usar - to use, wear
viajar - to travel

ER Verbs: (correr)

1. –o
2. –és
3. –e
4. –emos
5. –en

corr*o* - I run
corr*és* - you run
corr*e* - he/she runs, you run
corr*emos* - we run
corr*en* - they run, you all run

Other regular –er verbs:

aprender - to learn
beber - to drink
comer - to eat
comprender - to understand
correr - to run
coser – to sew
creer - to believe
leer - to read
toser – to cough
vender - to sell

IR Verbs: (vivir)

1. -o
2. -ís
3. -e
4. -imos
5. -en

viv*o* - I live
viv*ís* - you live
viv*e* - he/she lives, you live
viv*imos* - we live
viv*en* - they live, you all live

Other regular –ir verbs:

abrir - to open
compartir - to share
decidir - to decide
escribir - to write
recibir - to receive
vivir - to live

Irregular Verbs in the Present Tense

<u>Note</u>: Any verb in the present tense which deviates from these patterns is considered to be **irregular***. In previous chapters, you have already encountered some irregular verbs:

ser (to be)
estar (to be)
tener (to have)
hay (there is, there are)
ir (to go)
venir (to come)
llover – to rain
nevar – to snow
poder – can, to be able

Here are some other common irregular or stem-changing verbs:

conocer (to know people)
conozco
conocés
conoce
conocemos
conocen

dar (to give)
doy
das
da
damos
dan

---

*Some verbs such as *llover, nevar, doler* and *poder* are referred to as **stem-changing** verbs, rather than irregular verbs even though they deviate from the regular pattern.

decir (to say, tell)
digo
decís
dice
decimos
dicen

dormir (to sleep)
duermo
dormís
duerme
dormimos
duermen

jugar (to play sports)
juego
jugás
juega
jugamos
juegan

morir (to die)
muero
morís
muere
morimos
meuren

ofrecer (to offer)
ofrezco
ofrecés
ofrece
ofrecemos
ofrecen

oír (to hear)
oigo
oís
oye
oímos
oyen

preferir (to prefer)
prefiero
preferís
prefiere
preferimos
prefieren

querer (to want)
quiero
querés
quiere
queremos
quieren

saber (to know)
sé
sabés
sabe
sabemos
saben

salir (to leave, go out)
salgo
salís
sale
salimos
salen

traer (to bring)
traigo
traés
trae
traemos
traen

venir (to come)
vengo
venís
viene
venimos
vienen

Regular Verbs in the Preterite Tense
(the simple past tense)

AR Verbs: (bailar)
1. –é
2. –aste
3. – ó
4. –amos
5. –aron

bail*é* - I danced
bail*aste* - you danced
bail*ó* - he/she danced, you danced
bail*amos* - we danced
bail*aron* - they danced, you all danced

ER/IR Verbs: (correr)*
1. –í
2. –iste
3. –ió
4. –imos
5. –ieron

corr*í* - I ran
corr*iste* - you ran
corr*ió* - he/she ran, you ran
corr*imos* - we ran
corr*ieron* - they ran, you all ran

*Notice that the verb endings for *–er* and *–ir* verbs are the **same** in the preterite.

There are also many **irregular verbs** in the preterite tense. Here are some common ones. Notice that, unlike regular verbs, none of these forms has accent marks:

tener (to have): tuve, tuviste, tuvo, tuvimos, tuvieron
estar (to be): estuve, estuviste, estuvo, estuvimos, estuvieron
andar (to walk): anduve, anduviste, anduvo, anduvimos, anduvieron
venir (to come): vine, viniste, vino, vinimos, vinieron
querer (to want): quise, quisiste, quiso, quisimos, quisieron
hacer (to do, to make): hice, hiciste, hizo, hicimos, hicieron
poder (to be able, can): pude, pudiste, pudo, pudimos, pudieron
poner (to put): puse, pusiste, puso, pusimos, pusieron
saber (to know): supe, supiste, supo, supimos, supieron
caber (to fit): cupe, cupiste, cupo, cupimos, cupieron

The verbs **ir** (to go) and **ser** (to be) have the **same verb forms** in the preterite tense. This sharing of forms occurs with **no other verbs** and in **no other tense/mood** with these two verbs:

fui - I was, I went
fuiste - you were, you went
fue - he/she was, he/she went, you were, you went (formal)
fuimos - we were, we went
fueron - they were, they went/you all were, you all went

The Imperfect Tense

Regular Verb Endings in the Imperfect Tense

ar verbs: -aba, -abas, -aba, -ábamos, -aban
er/ir verbs: -ía, -ías, -ía, -íamos, -ían

The imperfect tense is used to talk about events which happened in the past on a regular basis or over an indefinite time period (e.g. *I used to work, I would work*). It also sometimes conveys what would be the past continuous in English (e.g. *I was working* instead of *I worked*). Notice that **forms 1 and 3 have the same endings** which means that sometimes it is recommendable to use the optional pronouns *yo* (I), *él* (he), *ella* (she) or *usted* (you formal) to avoid confusion regarding who is the subject of the verb.

The imperfect tense has **only three irregular verbs** which are as follows:

ir (to go): iba, ibas, iba, íbamos, iban
ser (to be): era, eras, era, éramos, eran
ver (to see): veía, veías, veía, veíamos, veían

The Present and Past Perfect Tenses

For the **present perfect** and **past perfect** (or *pluperfect*) tenses, you will use the appropriate form of the helping verb *haber* (to have) along with the **past participle** which is formed by removing the *-ar*, *-er* or *-ir* ending from the infinitive form of a verb and adding the following endings: –ado (ar verbs) and –ido (er/ir verbs). For example:

hablar = to speak
hablado = spoken
he hablado = I have spoken
había hablado = I had spoken

comer = to eat
comido = eaten
he comido = I have eaten
había comido = I had eaten

vivir = to live
vivido = lived
he vivido = I have lived
había vivido = I had lived

Here are the forms of the helping verb *haber*:

present perfect tense: *he, has, ha, hemos, han*

past perfect/pluperfect tense: *había, habías, había, habíamos, habían*

Here is an example of the forms in the present and past perfect of the verb *hablar* (to speak):

he hablado - I have spoken
has hablado – you have spoken
ha hablado – he/she has spoken
hemos hablado – we have spoken
han hablado – they/you all have spoken

había hablado - I had spoken
habías hablado – you had spoken
había hablado – he/she had spoken
habíamos hablado – we had spoken
habían hablado – they/you all had spoken

The following verbs have irregular participles:

abrir (open): *abierto*
decir (say/tell): *dicho*
descubrir (discover): *descubierto*
escribir (write): *escrito*
hacer (do/make): *hecho*
poner (put): *puesto*
resolver (solve/resolve): *resuelto*
romper (break): *roto*
soltar (release/let go): *suelto*
ver (see): *visto*
volver/devolver (return): *vuelto/devuelto*

The Verb *haber*

The verb **haber** also has a single form that is used for each tense/mood:

hay = there is, there are
hubo/había = there was, there were
ha habido = there has been/there have been
había habido = there had been
habrá = there will be
habría = there would be
va a haber = there's going to be/there are going to be

The Future Tense and the Conditional Mood

In order to form the **future tense** and the **conditional mood**, you must add the following endings to the *infinitive* form of a verb:

future tense: -é, -ás, -á, -emos, -án
conditional mood: -ía, -ías, -ía, -íamos, -ían

hablar - to speak
hablaré - I will speak
hablarás - you will speak
hablará - he/she will speak, you will speak
hablaremos - we will speak
hablarán - they will speak/you all will speak

hablaría - I would speak
hablarías - you would speak
hablaría - he/she would speak, you would speak
hablaríamos - we would speak
hablarían - they/you all would speak

The following verbs use irregular stems to form the *future* and *conditional* instead of the infinitive:

caber (to fit):	cabr-
decir (to say, tell):	dir-
hacer (to do, make):	har-
poner (to put):	pondr-
querer (to want):	querr-
saber (to know):	sabr-
salir (to leave, go out):	saldr-
tener (to have):	tendr-
valer (to be worth):	valdr-
venir (to come):	vendr-

Verb Forms and Constructions

trabaj**o** - I work./I'm working
no trabaj**o** - I don't work/I'm not working

estoy trabaj**ando** - I'm working (at this moment or on a regular basis)

trabaj**é** - I worked (completed action or for a definite time period)
trabaj**aba** - I was working/I used to work/I would work (habitually/on a regular basis)

no trabaj**é** - I didn't work
no trabaj**aba** - I wasn't working/I didn't used to work

voy a trabajar - I'm going to work

trabajaré - I will work
trabajaría - I would work (conditional - not in the past)

he trabaj**ado** - I have worked
había trabaj**ado** - I had worked (or less commonly *hube trabajado*)

estaba trabaj**ando**/**estuve** trabaj**ando** - I was working (act in progress)
estaré trabaj**ando** - I will be working
trabaj**aba**/**solía** trabaj**ar** - I used to work (previously, but not anymore)

debo trabaj**ar**/**debería** trabaj**ar** - I should work/I ought to work/I must work
tengo que trabaj**ar** - I have to work/I must work

he estado trabaj**ando** - I have been working
había estado trabaj**ando** - I had been working

¡Trabajá! - Work! (vos)
¡No trabajes! - Don't work! (vos)

¡Trabaje! - Work! (usted)
¡No trabaje! - Don't work! (usted)

¡Trabajen! - Work! (ustedes)
¡No trabajen! - Don't work! (ustedes)

¡Vamos a trabajar!/¡Trabajemos! - Let's work!
¡No vamos a trabajar!/¡No trabajemos! - Let's not work!

Important Words

la mañana - morning
la tarde - afternoon
la noche - night/evening

pronto - soon/quickly/early
temprano - early
a tiempo - on time
tarde - late

la hora - hour, time (of the clock)
ahora - now
el horario - schedule

solamente - only
sólo - only
solo - alone

no - no, not

y - and (e before a word which begins
            with i or hi)
o - or (u before a word which begins
            with o or ho)

con - with
sin - without
conmigo - with me
contigo/con vos - with you (familiar)

la cosa - the thing
las cosas - the things, things

algo - something
nada - nothing, not anything

alguien - someone
nadie - no one, not anyone

algún/alguno - some
ningún/ninguno - none, not any

pero - but
sino - but rather, but instead

muy - very
mucho - a lot, much, often (adverb)
poco - little, a little (adverb)

Bueno.../Pues... - Well,... (pause word)

mucho/mucha - a lot, much (adjective)
muchos/muchas - a lot of, many (adj.)

poco/poca - little (adjective)
pocos/pocas - few (adjective)

todo - all, everything
todos - all, everyone

cada - each
tal vez/quizá(s) - maybe, perhaps

primero - first
entonces - then
luego - later
antes (de) - before
después (de) - after
por fin - finally

nuevo - new
viejo - old

joven - young
viejo - old

mismo - same
distinto/diferente - different
otro - other, another

muy - very

más - more, most
menos - minus, less, least
más que/más de - more than (*de* is used before numbers, e.g. *más de 50*)
menos que/menos de - less than

mayor que - older than
menor que - younger than

mejor que - better than
peor que - worse than
mejor - better, best
peor - worse, worst

81

tan...como... - as...as...
tanto como... - as much as...

hay - there is, there are
hay que + infinitive - one must...

fácil - easy
difícil - hard, difficult

durante – during
mientras – while/whilst

la verdad - the truth
¿verdad?/¿no? - Right?

ya - already
ya no - no more, no longer, not anymore

todavía/aún - still, yet

siempre – always
nunca – never
a veces − sometimes
normalmente – usually
a menudo – often
rara vez/raras veces – rarely

Adjectives of Feelings and Conditions
(often used with the verb **estar***)

feliz/contento – happy/content
triste – sad
emocionado/ilusionado – excited
deprimido – depressed
aburrido – bored (this means *boring* when used with the verb **ser**)
cansado – tired
enfermo – sick
fastidiado/irritado – annoyed/irritated
enojado/enfadado – angry
alterado/molesto – upset
harto – fed up
decepcionado/desilusionado – disappointed
desanimado – discouraged
relajado – relaxed
tranquilo – calm
listo – ready, prepared
nervioso - nervous
preocupado – worried
asustado – afraid, scared
loco – crazy

Slang Phrases:

estar en pedo – to be drunk
estar en pelotas – to be naked

*Some adjectives can also be used with the verb **ser** (e.g. *feliz, loco*) if it is considered a permanent trait or something other than just a temporary condition.

Tricky Words

Here are some words in Spanish which are similar in appearance to English words, but which have very different meanings:

Spanish Word	English Meaning
actual	current
actualmente	currently/at the present time
argumento	plot of story or argument in the sense of a point made
arma	gun or weapon
asistir	to attend (an event, class, etc.)
atender	to serve/to wait on/to attend to
avisar	to warn, to give (advance) notice
bigote	moustache
bombero	fireman/firefighter
campo	field
carácter	moral character or temper, but **not** person in story, etc.
cartón	cardboard
colegio	high school or elementary school
collar	necklace
comer	to eat
compromiso	commitment
confiar	to trust
contar	*to count*, but also *to tell* in the sense of *to relate* or *recount* an event or something that took place
contestar	to answer
copa	goblet (*tomar una copa* = to have a drink)
crudo	raw
cuestión	question (only in the sense of *issue* or *point*)
decepción	disappointment

84

Spanish Word English Meaning

Spanish Word	English Meaning
decepcionar	to disappoint
delito	crime
demandar	to sue
discusión (fuerte)	argument (i.e. between two or more people)
discutir	this means "argue" more and "discuss" less
disgusto	displeasure
disgustar	to displease/to upset
educación	education (but also "upbringing", i.e. how you were raised)
embarazada	pregnant
embarazar	to get someone pregnant
emocionado	excited
emocionante	thrilling
éxito	success, hit (song)
forma	form, but also *shape* and *form* in the sense of *way/mode*
frustrar	*frustrate*, but also *thwart*
ganga	bargain/good deal
guardar	keep or put away (but not *guard*)
globo	balloon
ilusión	hope(s), dreams, excited expectation
largo	long
librería	book store/book shop
molesto	upset
molestar	to bother, upset, annoy
norma	rule, policy, standard
oficio	trade or profession (*oficina/despacho* = office)

Spanish Word English Meaning

Spanish Word	English Meaning
planta	plant, but also story of a building and sole of foot
pretender	to attempt, to claim
real	real (but also "royal")
realizar	to realize (but only in the sense of realizing a dream, etc.)
receta	kitchen recipe or prescription for medicine
recuerdo	memory, souvenir
recordar	to remember, to remind
reunión	meeting or get-together
sano	healthy, wholesome, intact
sensible	sensitive
simpático	nice (personality), easy-going
soportar	bear, stand, endure
suceso	event/happening
taller	workshop/garage
tiempo	time, but *also* weather
varios	several

Grammatical Differences

El Voseo

This is the most obvious difference between Spanish as it's spoken in Argentina (as well as Uruguay and Paraguay) and Spanish as it's spoken in other parts of the world.

This refers to the use of the singular, pronoun *vos* instead of the pronoun *tú* which is the second personal singular familiar form of address (i.e. *you* when you are speaking to one person who is your age or younger, who is a friend or member of your family).

I suppose that some people have the idea that Argentina is the only country that uses *vos* in this fashion. However, the truth is that most Latin American countries have (at least) a limited use of the pronoun *vos*, although there are many variations of how it is used. It's possible to travel to a country like Mexico or Peru and not be aware that small areas of those countries use the pronoun *vos*, since they don't include large cities or places where tourists typically go.

Argentina, Uruguay and Paraguay are the main countries where the use of *vos* is considered the norm in both written in spoken form.

The use of *vos* is also fairly widespread in most of Central America and in South America, especially in the Andean Mountain regions.

There are currently only three Spanish speaking countries where *vos* is **not used at all** which are: Spain, Puerto Rico and the Dominican Republic. Apparently, *vos* is used in parts of southeastern Cuba, although some believe that the practice is quickly dying out.

The use of *vos* should not be confused with the use of the plural pronoun *vosotros* which is only used in Spain.

In most countries, including those which do not use *vos* in modern usage, it is considered an archaic usage, the same way in which we consider the use of the pronouns *thee* and *thou* in English.

Although the use of *vos* varies in different countries, here is the way it is used in Argentina (and likely also Uruguay and Paraguay).

The verb forms of *vos* are only distinct in the **present simple indicative** and in **command** forms. That is to say, the verb forms are completely the same as in Standard Spanish in the *preterite, imperfect, future* tenses, etc.

In the Present Tense

For the *ser*:

vos sos (this is *tú eres* in Standard Spanish)

Other verbs in the Present Indictative:

For −**ar** and −**er** verbs, the form is the same, but with an accent mark on the *a* and *e* respectively. For example:

hablas→*hablás*

corres→*corrés*

Of course, the accent mark **affects the pronunciation** since you must stress the last (rather than the next to last) syllable.

For −**ir** verbs in the present indicative you must use −*is* which is identical to the vosotros form of −**ir** verbs in Spain. For example:

vives→vivís

Stem-Change Verbs

Verbs which normally have a stem-change in the present indicative, **do not** have the same change in Argentina. For example:

tienes→*tenés*
cierras→*cerrás*
quieres→*querés*
juegas→*jugás*

Apparently, the stem-changes are preserved in the *present subjunctive*. So you may see or hear:

Quiero que (vos) cierres la puerta. - I want you to shut the door.

In such a case, the stem-change may be preserved since we are dealing with the present subjunctive rather than the present indicative.

Commands

With regard to −**ar** and −**er** verbs, the difference is the same as in the present indicative, that is to say, you must add an accent on the *a* and *e* respectively. For example:

habla→*hablá*
corre→*corré*

Remember that this change also affects the pronunciation of the word.

For −**ir** verbs, the ending will be *–í*. For example:

escribe→*escribí*
ven→*vení*

The accent mark which is necessary to preserve the stressed syllable in Standard Spanish when adding a pronoun to the end of the word is **not necessary** in Argentina if you only add one pronoun.

háblame→*hablame*

This is because, you are actually putting the stress on the second to last syllable. However, if you add two pronouns, you will need an accent mark, but it won't be on the same syllable as in Standard Spanish. For example.

explícamelo→explicámelo

One other notable difference:

¡Vete!→*¡Andate!* (Go away!)

Pronunciation and Vocabulary Differences

Pronunciation

Argentine Spanish **shares two things in common** with Latin American pronunciation:

1. The pronunciation of *ce*, *ci* and *z* has an *ss* sound as in the word *class* rather than the *th* sound of the word *thin* as you will hear in most of Spain.

2. There exists the tendency in Buenos Aires and other coastal areas to "eat" or not pronounce the final *s* of a word, especially in informal speak. This tendency is also common in the Caribbean region of as well as in the coastal areas of South America.

The main difference in the pronunciation of Argentine (and also Uruguayan) Spanish compared with Standard Spanish, including Spanish as it's spoken in Spain, is regarding the pronunciation of the *ll* and the consonant *y*. These are both pronounced like the letter *y* in Standard Spanish (and similar to an English *j* in some regions, but this is not considered to be proper or standard Spanish). In Argentina and Uruguay, the *ll* and *y* are pronounced the *j* of French (that is to say like the *s* in the English word *measure*).

This pronunciation of the *y* apparently doesn't pertain the *y* at the end of a word (e.g. *soy*). However, it does affect the letter *y* as the first letter of a word (e.g. *yo*) or between vowels (e.g. *vaya*), and it affects the pronunciation of the *ll* in all cases, since words in Spanish do not typically end with *ll* (e.g. *ella*, *llorar*).

Therefore, if you are thinking of how a *j* is pronounced in French, then *yo me llamo* (my name is) will sound like *jo* me *j*amo (or if you are thinking of the *s* of *measure*, like *s*o me *s*amo).

Vocabulary Differences:

Loan Words

Argentine Spanish contains loan words from other languages; especially English, French and Italian. For example:

living (room), *shopping* (center)
placard, can-can (from French)
gamba, birra (from Italian)

Argentine Slang

Argentine slang is known as *lunfardo*, and is apparently widespread in usage, although its origins were apparently from the lower classes and also having some connection to tango music or dancing. This slang may also have originally had some connection to the Argentine underworld or criminal elements. Although this book may contain a few slang words, I prefer not to treat this subject in this book. For this I will recommend that the reader look for specialized books on this subject, and there is likely much information on this topic available on the internet.

Alternative Terms

In some cases, Argentines may use unique words as an alternative for a standard Spanish word. For example:

gamba for leg (pierna)
birra for beer (cerveza)
campera for jacket (chaqueta)

Here are some other common words that are unique to Argentine (and perhaps also to Uruguayan) Spanish:

Home and Places
el *living* – living room (sala, salón)
el *placard* – closet/wardrobe (armario)
el *shopping* – shopping center (centro comercial)
el *velador* – lamp (lámpara)
la bacha – bathroom sink (lavabo, lavamanos)
la *frasada* – blanket (manta)
la *pileta* – kitchen sink (pila, fregadero)
la *pileta* – swimming pool (piscina)

School and Office
la *birome* – pen (bolígrafo)
la *lapicera* - pen (possibly also used in other countries)

Clothes
el *buzo* – sweatshirt (sudadera)
los *can-can* – pantyhose, tights (medias)
la *campera* – jacket (chaqueta)
la *malla* – swimsuit (traje de baño)
la *pollera* – skirt (falda)
la *remera* – T-shirt (camiseta)
las *medias* – socks (calcetines)

Food
la *factura* – sweetroll, bun (pan dulce, bollo)
las *masitas* – cookies, biscuits (galletas)
el *pancho* – hotdog (perro caliente)
las *arvejas* – peas (guisantes, chícharos)
las *chauchas* – green beans (judías verdes, ejotes)

54245136R00061

Made in the USA
Lexington, KY
07 August 2016